2nd Grade Reading Comprehension Book

Over 100 activities to improve reading, comprehension in struggling readers. A powerful resource for parents, teachers and educators. Decodable books for decodable readers.

BrainChild

Introduction

Teaching a child with dyslexia to read: Dyslexia is a specific and persistent learning disability that affects reading and writing. Teaching a child with dyslexia to read and write can become a difficult challenge for families and educators to tackle. For these children, written language becomes a great barrier, often without meaning or logic, which generates rejection of the task, frustration and discomfort.
A child with dyslexia has significant difficulties in these areas because their brain processes information differently than other children, which is why if we expect the same results following the traditional method, we will find many barriers that can and often do harm the child. It is important to become aware of the areas where the child struggles, to help them overcome these difficulties and make reading an easier task.

Reading difficulties with dyslexia

Dyslexia is a neurobiological disorder that affects the development and structuring of certain areas of the brain. Therefore, it causes the brain to process information differently, making it difficult for the person to understand letters, their sounds, their combinations, etc.

Human language is a language based on signs, letters and their sounds, which are arbitrary. The relationship between each grapheme (letter) with its phoneme (sound), does not follow any logic; it's simply chance. This is one of the greatest difficulties that children face when they have to learn to read and write. Converting spoken language into signs and symbols, and transforming sounds into letters, is a challenge. This is even more complicated in children with dyslexia; the relationship becomes something indecipherable for them. No matter how hard they try, they cannot make sense of that dance between letters and sounds.

Children with dyslexia have trouble recognizing letters, sometimes they mistake letters for others, write them backwards, etc. They also have a hard time knowing the sound that corresponds to each letter; and things get even more complicated when we combine several letters and we have to know several sounds. Learning new words is also a challenge and they can easily forget them, so it's important that the child works hard to acquire them. Sometimes they read certain words effortlessly, but the next day they completely forget them. When they write, they omit letters, change their position, forget words in a sentence, etc.

Dyslexia also affects reading comprehension. When reading, they are trying really hard to decipher and understand each word, sometimes even each letter; that is why the meaning of the text gets lost.

Activities to help develop reading comprehension in children

How to teach a child with dyslexia to read:

A child with dyslexia has difficulty learning to read and write, because it is hard for them to recognize letters and know which sound, they correspond to. However, the child can learn to overcome those difficulties. Remember that dyslexia is a learning difficulty that does not imply any physical or mental handicap; the child with dyslexia has adequate capacities. In order to teach a child with dyslexia to read, it is essential to know the nature of their difficulties, understand them and use a teaching method that responds to their needs.

A teaching method to help the child read:

In the first place, it is necessary to assess the child's reading and writing level and the nature and characteristics of their difficulties, so as to understand their specific needs. For this, it's advisable to seek a specialist. Reading favors the development of phonological awareness (which consists of the letter-sound correspondence). To do this, start with simple activities, letter by letter, even if other children around the same age read full texts. Later, we can continue with full words, phrases and texts. It is about dedicating more time and more detail to the learning process.

Phonological awareness worksheets

Use motivational activities that are engaging. Do not limit the child to just paper and pencil: they can make letters out of play dough, write on sand with their fingers, play catch or games such as hangman, word searches, crossword puzzles, etc. Don't force them to read or read a lot. Try to have them read on a daily basis, little by little; sometimes a sentence or a paragraph is enough. Help them understand what they read, ask them questions, ask them to read again, etc.

Copyright 2024 - All Rights Reserved

Contents of this book may not be reproduced, duplicated or transmitted without direct written permission from the author. Under no circumstances will any legal responsibility or blame be held against the publisher for any reparation, damages or monetary loss due to information herein, either directly o indirectly.

Legal Notice:

You cannot amend, distribute, sell, use, quote or paraphrase any part of the contents within this book without the consent of the author.

Disclaimer note:

Please note that the information contained within this document serves only for educational and entertainment purposes. No warranties of any kind are expressed or implied. Readers acknowledge that the author is not engaging in the rendering of legal, financial, medical or professional advice.

Table of Contents

'a' words activities ……………………… page 1-20

'e' words activities ………………….. page 21-40

'i' words activities ………………… page 41-60

'o' words activities ………………….. page 61-80

'u' words activities ………………… page 81-100

Read the story and circle the 'a' words. Write the 'a' words in the box given below.

A Playful Picnic

Once upon a time, Sam and Pam went for a stroll in the park. The sun was shining, and they decided to have a picnic. As they unpacked their bag, Sam noticed a shiny pan hidden inside. Pam bragged about her cooking skills and offered to make some delicious pancakes.

While they cooked, a little girl sat nearby with her father, watching in awe. The man wore a tan hat and held a fan to keep himself cool. Suddenly, a strong gust of wind blew, and the flag on top of a nearby hill began to flap vigorously.

Sam and Pam enjoyed their meal, feeling glad to be outside on such a beautiful day. After eating, they played catch with a small rag ball, throwing it with a red tag attached. Sam swung the bat to hit the ball, but accidentally knocked off his hat. As he laughed, Pam joined in, realizing they were having so much fun.

The day ended as they walked back home, pushing a blue pram filled with memories and a jar of sweet strawberry jam.

Write all the 'a' words found in the story.

Read the story "A Playful Picnic" and answer the questions asked below.

Questions and Answers

Who were the main characters in the story?
_____
_____
_____

What did Sam and Pam find hidden inside their bag?
_____
_____
_____

What activity did Sam and Pam decide to do after their picnic?
_____
_____
_____

What color was the hat that Sam was wearing?
_____
_____
_____

What did Sam accidentally knock off while playing catch?
_____
_____
_____

Read the story "A Playful Picnic" and answer the questions asked below by choosing the correct option.

Multiple Choice Questions

What did Sam and Pam find hidden inside their bag?

a) A shiny pan

b) A colorful kite

c) A set of playing cards

What activity did Sam and Pam decide to do after their picnic?

a) Fly a kite

b) Play catch

c) Build sandcastles

What color was the hat that Sam was wearing?

a) Tan

b) Red

c) Blue

What did Sam accidentally knock off while playing catch?

a) His hat

b) The rag ball

c) Pam's sunglasses

Who were the main characters in the story?

a) Sam and Pam

b) Jack and Jill

c) Tom and Sarah

Read the story "A Playful Picnic" and solve the exercises given below.

Fill in the blanks

Sam and Pam went on a picnic _____.

They packed a basket full of delicious _____.

As they unpacked, they discovered a surprise _____ inside their bag.

Sam and Pam decided to have a game of _____ after their picnic.

The weather was perfect with clear blue skies and a gentle _____ blowing.

Sam wore a bright _____ hat to protect himself from the sun.

Pam brought her favorite _____ to enjoy during the picnic.

While playing catch, Sam accidentally knocked off his _____.

They laughed and enjoyed the playful _____ during their picnic.

It was a memorable day filled with laughter, delicious food, and special _____.

True or False

Sam and Pam went on a picnic.	(True / False)
They discovered a surprise gift inside their bag.	(True / False)
Sam wore a red hat to protect himself from the sun.	(True / False)
They played catch during their picnic.	(True / False)
Sam accidentally knocked off Pam's sunglasses while playing catch.	(True / False)
Sam and Pam enjoyed flying a kite after their picnic.	(True / False)
The weather during their picnic was rainy and stormy.	(True / False)
Sam and Pam found a shiny pan hidden inside their bag.	(True / False)

Read the story "A Playful Picnic" then read the statements written below and rewrite the correct statements.

Rewrite the correct statements

Sam and Pam went for a walk in the forest instead of the park.
_____

The weather was gloomy and rainy, not sunny.
_____

Instead of pancakes, Pam cooked scrambled eggs for their picnic.
_____

The man wore a blue hat, not a tan one.
_____

The gust of wind blew the flag on top of a building, not a hill.
_____

Sam and Pam played soccer with a football, not catch with a rag ball.
_____

Sam accidentally knocked off Pam's hat, not his own.
_____

Instead of laughing, Pam got angry at Sam for knocking off her hat.
_____

They didn't have a jar of strawberry jam, but a jar of peanut butter.
_____

Read the story and circle the 'am' words. Write the 'am' words in the box given below.

A Day with Sam and Pam

Once upon a time, Sam and Pam took their baby for a walk in the park. They pushed the blue pram along the path, enjoying the fresh air. As they strolled, they came across a small dam with ducks swimming happily. Sam pointed at the ducks, making their baby giggle with delight.

Feeling hungry, they decided to find a spot for a picnic. Pam unpacked a delicious ham sandwich and some crunchy clam chips. Sam brought out a jar of homemade strawberry jam to spread on their sandwiches. The sweet aroma filled the air, attracting a curious squirrel.

After their meal, they hopped on a tram to explore the city. The tram rattled along, passing colorful buildings and bustling streets. They even saw a street performer playing the ram's horn, adding a touch of music to their journey.

As they returned home, they realized they had fallen victim to a scam. Someone had stolen their wallets while they were on the tram. Despite the setback, they were grateful for the wonderful day they had spent together, and they knew that memories were worth more than any material possession.

Write all the 'am' words found in the story.

Read the story "A Day with Sam and Pam" and answer the questions asked below.

Questions and Answers

What color was the pram that Sam and Pam pushed along the path?
_____
_____
_____

What did Pam unpack for their picnic?
_____
_____
_____

What did Sam bring out from a jar to spread on their sandwiches?
_____
_____
_____

What did they see a street performer playing while on the tram?
_____
_____
_____

What unfortunate event happened to Sam and Pam while they were on the tram?
_____
_____
_____

Read the story "A Day with Sam and Pam" and answer the questions asked below by choosing the correct option.

Multiple Choice Questions

What color was the pram that Sam and Pam pushed along the path?

a) Red

b) Blue

c) Green

What did Pam unpack for their picnic?

a) Chicken sandwich

b) Ham sandwich

c) Cheese sandwich

What did Sam bring out from a jar to spread on their sandwiches?

a) Peanut butter

b) Mustard

c) Strawberry jam

What did they see a street performer playing while on the tram?

a) Saxophone

b) Guitar

c) Ram's horn

What unfortunate event happened to Sam and Pam while they were on the tram?

a) They lost their wallets

b) They missed their stop

c) The tram broke down

Read the story "A Day with Sam and Pam" and solve the exercises given below.

Fill in the blanks

Sam and Pam took a leisurely stroll along the _____.

Pam unpacked a colorful _____ for their picnic.

Sam spread a generous amount of _____ on their sandwiches.

They spotted a talented _____ playing music on the tram.

Unfortunately, Sam and Pam accidentally left their _____ at home.

The weather was perfect, with clear blue skies and a gentle _____.

They sat on a _____ to enjoy their delicious picnic lunch.

Pam brought along her favorite book, _____, to read during their outing.

Sam and Pam laughed as they watched children flying _____ in the park.

Sam and Pam had a wonderful day filled with laughter and _____.

True or False

Sam and Pam took their baby for a walk in the park. (True / False)

They pushed a blue pram along the path. (True / False)

They came across a small dam with ducks swimming happily. (True / False)

Sam pointed at the ducks, making their baby giggle with delight. (True / False)

Pam unpacked a delicious ham sandwich and some crunchy clam chips. (True / False)

A squirrel was attracted by the sweet aroma of the strawberry jam. (True / False)

After their meal, they hopped on a tram to explore the city. (True / False)

While on the tram, they saw a street performer playing the ram's horn. (True / False)

Read the story "A Day with Sam and Pam" then read the statements written below and rewrite the correct statements.

Rewrite the correct statements.

Sam and Pam took their dog for a walk in the park instead of their baby.
_____

They pushed a red pram along the path, not a blue one.
_____

The ducks they came across were swimming sadly, not happily.
_____

It was Pam who pointed at the ducks, not Sam.
_____

Instead of a ham sandwich, Pam unpacked a turkey sandwich.
_____

Sam brought out a jar of store-bought strawberry jam, not homemade.
_____

The sweet aroma of the strawberry jam did not attract any curious squirrel.
_____

They decided to hop on a bus, not a tram, to explore the city.
_____

Their wallets were stolen before they got on the tram, not while they were on it.
_____

Read the story and circle the 'an' words. Write the 'an' words in the box given below.

Stan's Van

In a small town, there lived a man named Stan. He had a trusty old van that he used for all his adventures. Stan was a resourceful man who always had a plan. With the flip of a pan and a can of paint, he transformed his van from a dull tan to a vibrant blue.

One day, as Stan drove through the town, he noticed a commotion up ahead. He parked his van and ran towards the crowd to scan the situation. It appeared that a ban had been placed on street performances, leaving the local artists in dismay.

Stan, being part of a creative clan, knew he had to help. He came up with a brilliant plan to organize a street festival where artists could showcase their talents. With his van serving as the stage, the event spanned across the entire town.

The festival was a tremendous success, bringing more joy to the community than anyone could imagine. Stan realized that there is more to life than just the material possessions his van represented. It was the connections, creativity, and love he shared that truly mattered.

Write all the 'an' words found in the story.

Read the story "Stan's Van" and answer the questions asked below.

Questions and Answers

How did Stan transform his tan van into a vibrant blue?
_____
_____
_____
_____

What prompted Stan to run towards the crowd in the town?
_____
_____
_____
_____

What was the problem that the ban imposed on street performances caused in the community?
_____
_____
_____
_____

How did Stan's plan to organize a street festival help the local artists?
_____
_____
_____
_____

What was more important than the material possessions Stan's van represented?
_____
_____

Read the story "Stan's Van" and answer the questions asked below by choosing the correct option.

Multiple Choice Questions

What color did Stan transform his van into?

a) Red

b) Blue

c) Green

Why did Stan run towards the crowd in the town?

a) To scan the situation

b) To buy some groceries

c) To meet a friend

What problem did the ban on street performances cause in the community?

a) Lack of entertainment options

b) Increased crime rates

c) Traffic congestion

How did Stan's plan to organize a street festival help the local artists?

a) It provided them with a platform to showcase their talents

b) It offered them free transportation in his van

c) It gave them access to new art supplies

What did Stan realize was more important than material possessions?

a) Fame and fortune

b) Creativity and community connections

c) Luxury and comfort

Read the story "Stan's Van" and solve the exercises given below.

Fill in the blanks

Stan's _____ van caught everyone's attention as it rolled down the street.

He spent days transforming the van from a dull color to a vibrant shade of _____.

The ban left the community devoid of _____ and artistic expression.

Stan's plan to organize a street festival aimed to bring back the sense of _____ in the neighborhood.

Local artists eagerly joined Stan's cause, excited for the opportunity to showcase their _____.

As the festival kicked off, the streets were filled with music, laughter, and a _____ atmosphere.

Stan realized that the true value of his van lay not in its appearance, but in the _____ it created.

True or False

Stan's van was originally colored tan. (True / False)

Stan transformed his van into a vibrant blue color. (True / False)

Stan's plan to organize a street festival aimed to promote local artists. (True / False)

The street festival brought music, laughter, and a festive atmosphere to the neighborhood. (True / False)

Stan realized that material possessions were more important than community connections. (True / False)

The festival served as a reminder of the importance of unity within a community.

(True / False)

Read the story "Stan's Van" then read the statements written below and rewrite the correct statements.

Rewrite the correct statements.

Stan's van was originally colored pink.
_____

Stan transformed his van into a dull shade of gray.
_____

The ban on street performances had no impact on the community.
_____

Stan's plan to organize a street festival aimed to discourage local artists.
_____

The street festival brought silence and boredom to the neighborhood.
_____

Stan realized that material possessions were more important than community connections.
_____

The festival served as a reminder of the division within the community.
_____

People from different backgrounds boycotted the street festival.
_____

Stan's van remained unnoticed and unseen by everyone.
_____

Use the words given below in your own sentences.

Sentences

Bat: _____
Hat: _____
Mat: _____
Rat: _____
Fat: _____
Bag: _____
Rag: _____
Flag: _____
Brag: _____
Drag: _____
Ban: _____
Fan: _____
Man: _____
Can: _____
Ran: _____
Ham: _____
Ram: _____
Dam: _____

Identify the picture and write its name.

Match the picture to its name.

Mat

Stag

Pram

Bag

Van

Fan

Flag

Can

Hat

Rat

Jam

ham

Complete the word by looking at the picture.

 🛒	pr	a	m	pram
 🎒	b			
 🚐	v			
 🌀	f			
 🥩	h			
 🍓	j			
🥤	c			
🦌	st			

Find and circle the words written below.

ham fan can ban flag rag brag van tan man mat sat cat

v	t	a	n	m	a	t	f
a	m	a	n	n	a	f	r
n	c	a	t	s	y	v	a
w	w	i	e	r	a	e	i
s	f	a	m	b	l	n	g
r	y	a	e	j	a	a	a
a	h	b	n	c	p	n	l
g	b	r	a	g	l	s	f

Read the story and circle the 'e' words. Write the 'e' words in the box given below.

Ted's Adventures

Once upon a time, there was a teddy bear named Ted. Ted had soft, red fur and a friendly smile stitched on his face. He lived on a cozy bed in a child's room. Every night, the child would tuck Ted into bed and read him a bedtime story.

One day, Ted decided to explore beyond the confines of his bed. He hopped off and found himself tangled in a net. Luckily, a kind little girl named Ben rescued him and set him free.

Grateful for her help, Ted befriended Ben and they embarked on adventures together. They made a bet to see who could collect the most colorful leaves in the park. Ted led the way, using his sharp eyes to spot the brightest hues.

As they gathered leaves, a mischievous hen chased them. Ted and Ben ran, but the hen's friends, a group of noisy men, joined the chase. Ted, being small, slipped through a hole in a fence and escaped.

Safe and sound, Ted met a clever fox named Pen. Pen showed Ted a secret hideaway with a majestic view. Ted realized that he had found his perfect spot to relax and let his imagination roam free.

From that day on, Ted and Pen spent their days enjoying the beauty of nature, leaving behind the worries of the world.

Write all the 'e' words found in the story.

Read the story "Ted's Adventures" and answer the questions asked below.

Questions and Answers

What color was Ted's fur?

_____
_____
_____

Who rescued Ted when he got tangled in a net?

_____
_____
_____

What did Ted and Ben bet on in the park?

_____
_____
_____

Who chased Ted and Ben in the park?

_____
_____
_____

Who did Ted meet and befriend after escaping from the chase?

_____
_____
_____

Read the story "Ted's Adventures" and answer the questions asked below by choosing the correct option.

Multiple Choice Questions

What color was Ted's fur?

a) Blue

b) Red

c) Yellow

Who rescued Ted when he got tangled in a net?

a) Ben

b) Sam

c) Lily

What did Ted and Ben bet on in the park?

a) Who could collect the most colorful leaves

b) Who could climb the highest tree

c) Who could run the fastest

Who chased Ted and Ben in the park?

a) A hen

b) A squirrel

c) A rabbit

Who did Ted meet and befriend after escaping from the chase?

a) Pen the fox

b) Max the bear

c) Mia the cat

Read the story "Ted's Adventures" and solve the exercises given below.

Fill in the blanks

Ted's fur was a vibrant shade of _____.

When Ted got tangled in a net, it was _____ who came to the rescue.

In the park, Ted and Ben made a bet on who could collect the most _____ leaves.

As Ted and Ben were running, they were chased by a mischievous _____.

After escaping the chase, Ted met a friendly creature named _____.

Ted and Ben climbed up the tallest _____ in the park.

Ted's heart raced as he narrowly avoided a collision with a _____.

Ted's paws sank into the soft _____ as he explored a meadow.

Ted loved to hide among the colorful _____ in the forest.

Adventures beyond the bed opened up a world of _____ and excitement for Ted.

True or False

Ben rescued Ted when he got tangled in a net. (True / False)

Ted and Ben bet on who could collect the most flowers in the park. (True / False)

They were chased by a friendly bunny in the park. (True / False)

After escaping the chase, Ted met a grumpy bear. (True / False)

Ted and Ben climbed the tallest building in the park. (True / False)

Ted narrowly avoided a collision with a speeding car. (True / False)

Ted loved to hide among the colorful mushrooms in the forest. (True / False)

Read the story "Ted's Adventures" then read the statements written below and rewrite the correct statements.

Rewrite the correct statements.

Ted's fur was purple.
_____

It was Lily who rescued Ted when he got tangled in a net.
_____

In the park, Ted and Ben made a bet on who could collect the most seashells.
_____

They were chased by a ferocious lion in the park.
_____

After escaping the chase, Ted met a talking tree.
_____

Ted and Ben climbed up the tallest mountain in the park.
_____

Ted's heart raced as he narrowly avoided a collision with a spaceship.
_____

Ted's paws sank into the hard concrete as he explored a city.
_____

Ted loved to hide among the tall cacti in the desert.
_____

The adventures beyond the bed opened up a world of sadness and boredom for Ted.
_____

Read the story and circle the 'eg' words. Write the 'eg' words in the box given below.

Meg's Stellar Journey

Meg always dreamed of exploring the vast expanse of space as an astronaut. From a young age, she would beg her parents for books about the cosmos, plastering posters of rockets and stars on her bedroom walls. She was determined to soar beyond the limits of Earth.

But life had dealt Meg a difficult hand. A childhood accident left her with a prosthetic leg, and some people doubted she could chase her dreams. They would peg her as incapable, dismissing her ambitions. But Meg refused to be defined by her disability.

Undeterred, she pursued her passion relentlessly. She studied science and math, devouring knowledge like a thirsty man drinks from a keg. Despite the challenges, she excelled in her studies, earning the respect of her classmates and teachers.

One day, while volunteering at a local observatory, Meg caught the attention of Greg, a renowned astronaut. Impressed by Meg's determination and intellect, he became her mentor. Together, they embarked on a mission to prove that dreams and determination can overcome any obstacle.

Years later, Meg stood proudly as she boarded the spacecraft, ready to embark on her first interstellar journey. As the rocket roared to life, Meg smiled, knowing that her journey to the stars had just begun, fueled by a sprinkle of stardust and a pinch of nutmeg.

Write all the 'eg' words found in the story.

Read the story "Meg's Stellar Journey" and answer the questions asked below.

Questions and Answers

How did Meg's childhood accident affect her aspirations of becoming an astronaut?
_____
_____

Who doubted Meg's ability to pursue her dreams and how did she respond to their skepticism?
_____
_____

What subjects did Meg focus on in her studies to prepare for a career in space exploration?
_____
_____
_____

How did Meg catch the attention of Greg, the renowned astronaut, and what role did he play in her journey?
_____
_____

What emotions did Meg experience as she boarded the spacecraft for her first interstellar mission?
_____
_____

Read the story "Meg's Stellar Journey" and answer the questions asked below by choosing the correct option.

Multiple Choice Questions

What childhood incident did Meg overcome?

a) Broken arm

b) Prosthetic leg

c) Asthma

What subject did Meg excel in?

a) History

b) Science

c) Art

Who became Meg's mentor?

a) Her teacher

b) Her parent

c) Greg, a renowned astronaut

What did Meg volunteer for at the local observatory?

a) Cleaning duty

b) Data entry

c) Assisting with observations

How did Meg feel as she boarded the spacecraft?

a) Nervous

b) Angry

c) Excited

Read the story "Meg's Stellar Journey" and solve the exercises given below.

Fill in the blanks

Meg's childhood accident left her with a _____.

Despite the doubts of others, Meg was determined to become an _____.

Meg focused her studies on _____ and _____ to prepare for her space exploration career.

Greg, a renowned astronaut, noticed Meg's _____ and took her under his wing.

Meg volunteered at the local _____ to gain hands-on experience in astronomy.

As Meg boarded the spacecraft, a mix of _____ and _____ filled her heart.

Meg's journey took her _____ beyond the boundaries of Earth.

The weightlessness of space made Meg feel _____.

True or False

Meg's childhood accident hindered her dream of becoming an astronaut. (T/ F)

Meg faced skepticism from others regarding her ability to pursue her dreams. (T/ F)

Meg excelled in science and art during her studies. (T/ F)

Greg, a renowned astronaut, played a significant role in mentoring Meg. (T/ F)

Meg volunteered at the local observatory to gain practical experience in astronomy. (T/ F)

Meg felt a mix of nervousness and excitement as she boarded the spacecraft. (T/ F)

Meg's interstellar journey took her far beyond Earth's boundaries. (T/ F)

Meg's story inspired others to reach for their dreams in space exploration. (T/ F)

Read the story "Meg's Stellar Journey" then read the statements written below and rewrite the correct statements.

Rewrite the correct statements.

Meg's childhood accident left her with a broken leg.
_____

Meg decided to pursue a career in underwater exploration instead of space exploration.
_____

Meg struggled in her studies and had a hard time finding her passion.
_____

Greg, a renowned astronaut, didn't pay much attention to Meg.
_____

Meg volunteered at a local bakery instead of a local observatory.
_____

Meg felt absolutely no emotions as she boarded the spacecraft.
_____

Meg's interstellar journey took her only to the moon and back.
_____

The weightlessness of space made Meg feel extremely uncomfortable and sick.
_____

Meg didn't achieve any significant milestones in her space exploration career.
_____

Meg's story didn't inspire anyone and went unnoticed by others.
_____

Read the story and circle the 'en' words. Write the 'en' words in the box given below.

Ben's Camping Trip

Once upon a time, young Ben embarked on a camping adventure with his father. They ventured deep into a lush glen surrounded by towering trees. Excitement filled the air as they pitched their tent and prepared for a night under the stars.

As they settled in, Ben noticed a group of ten men nearby, gathering firewood. Intrigued, he approached them and struck up a conversation. To his surprise, one of the men mentioned spotting a rare wren nesting in a nearby fen. Eager to see this elusive bird, Ben couldn't wait for the morning to come.

When dawn broke, Ben and his father set out on a nature walk. Their path led them to the fen, where they spotted the wren's nest tucked away among the reeds. Nearby, a hen busily pecked at the ground, oblivious to their presence.

In that serene moment, Ben felt a sense of zen wash over him. He realized the true beauty of nature and the peaceful coexistence of its creatures.

With contentment in their hearts, they returned to their campsite, cherishing the memories made in the glen. And from that day forward, every time Ben heard the word "den," his mind would wander back to that magical camping trip.

Write all the 'en' words found in the story.

Read the story "Ben's Camping Trip" and answer the questions asked below.

Questions and Answers

What inspired Ben to approach the group of ten men during his camping trip?
_____
_____

What fascinating bird did the men discuss near the campsite, and where was its nest located?
_____
_____
_____

Where did Ben and his father come across a hen and her chicks during their nature walk?
_____
_____
_____

How did Ben feel when he observed the interactions of the hen and her chicks?
_____
_____
_____

What lasting impression did the camping trip leave on Ben in terms of appreciating nature and finding inner peace?
_____
_____

Read the story "Ben's Camping Trip" and answer the questions asked below by choosing the correct option.

Multiple Choice Questions

What type of bird did the men mention spotting in the fen?

a) Sparrow

b) Wren

c) Robin

How many men were in the group that Ben encountered near the campsite?

a) Five

b) Ten

c) Fifteen

Where was the wren's nest located?

a) Glen

b) Fen

c) Den

What animal did Ben and his father come across during their nature walk?

a) Rabbit

b) Hen

c) Squirrel

How did Ben feel when observing the hen and her chicks?

a) Excited

b) Scared

c) Content

Read the story "Ben's Camping Trip" and solve the exercises given below.

Fill in the blanks

Ben was _____ by the beauty of nature during his camping trip.

The group of men were discussing a rare bird they spotted in the _____.

Ben and his father stumbled upon a hen and her _____ during their nature walk.

The hen carefully _____ her chicks as they explored the surroundings.

Ben felt a sense of _____ as he observed the interactions between the hen and her chicks.

The men shared stories of their _____ adventures in the wild.

The wren's nest was hidden among the _____ trees near the campsite.

Ben was inspired to _____ the men and learn more about the bird they spotted.

The camping trip allowed Ben to connect with nature and find _____ within himself

True or False

Ben encountered a group of men during his camping trip. (True / False)

The men were discussing a rare bird they had spotted. (True / False)

The hen and her chicks were found near the campsite. (True / False)

The hen carefully watched over her chicks. (True / False)

Ben felt a sense of contentment while observing the hen and her chicks. (True / False)

The men shared stories about their adventures in the wild. (True / False)

The wren's nest was located in the fen. (True / False)

The camping trip helped Ben appreciate nature and find inner peace. (True / False)

Read the story "Ben's Camping Trip" then read the statements written below and rewrite the correct statements.

Rewrite the correct statements.

Ben encountered a group of women during his camping trip.
_____

The men were discussing a common bird they had spotted.
_____

The hen and her chicks were found near the river.
_____

The hen neglected her chicks as they explored the surroundings.
_____

Ben felt scared while observing the hen and her chicks.
_____

The men shared stories about their adventures in the city.
_____

The wren's nest was located in the tree.
_____

The camping trip made Ben dislike nature and feel restless.
_____

The glen was devoid of any wildlife.
_____

The experience in the glen had no impact on Ben's appreciation for the outdoors.
_____

Use the words given below in your own sentences.

Sentences

Bet: _____

Met: _____

Set: _____

Net: _____

Get: _____

Jet: _____

Beg: _____

Peg: _____

Leg: _____

Keg: _____

Hen: _____

Men: _____

Ben: _____

Wren: _____

Ten: _____

When: _____

Then: _____

Pen: _____

Identify the picture and write its name.

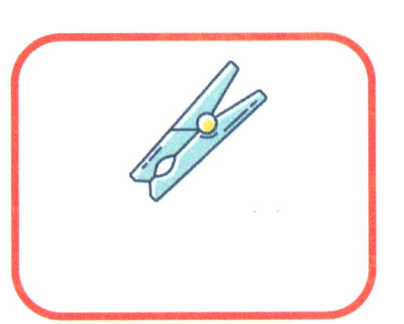

Match the picture to its name.

Bed

Pen

Den

Beg

Keg

Hen

Red

Peg

Yen

Ten

Net

Leg

Complete the word by looking at the picture.

	p			
	k			
	h			
	n			
	d			
	t			
	p			
	b			

Find and circle the words written below.

bed red net set get let jet beg peg leg
keg led Ted

k	t	d	n	m	a	t	l
a	e	a	t	e	d	f	e
l	c	g	t	s	y	v	g
w	w	i	e	r	a	e	p
s	f	a	m	s	l	g	e
r	y	a	r	e	e	j	g
a	h	n	e	t	p	e	e
g	b	e	d	l	e	t	b

Read the story and circle the 'i' words. Write the 'i' words in the box given below.

Chip's Treasure Hunt

Once upon a time, in a big farmyard, there lived a mischievous pig named Chip. Chip loved to explore and find hidden treasures. One day, while digging near the old rusty rig, he stumbled upon a tin box buried deep in the ground. Excitedly, Chip used his snout to pry open the lid, revealing a shiny golden coin.

Curiosity piqued, Chip wanted to share his discovery with his friends. He ran to the barn, where he found Flip the horse, Kit the kitten, and Pip the chicken knitting away. "Look what I found!", exclaimed Chip, showing them the golden coin. Their eyes widened in awe.

Together, they decided to embark on an adventure to find more treasures. They traveled far and wide, climbing trees, diving into rivers, and exploring caves. Along the way, they found a bin full of colorful figs, a hidden chest with a silver locket, and even a priceless ruby pendant.

Their excitement grew with each discovery. And so, Chip and his newfound friends continued their treasure hunt, cherishing the bonds they formed and the memories they created along the way.

Write all the 'i' words found in the story.

Read the story "Chip's Treasure Hunt" and answer the questions asked below.

Questions and Answers

Who is the mischievous character in the story?
_____
_____
_____

What did Chip find buried near the rusty rig?
_____
_____
_____

Which animals joined Chip on his treasure hunt?
_____
_____
_____

What were some of the treasures they discovered along their journey?
_____
_____
_____

What was the overall theme of the story?
_____
_____

Read the story "Chip's Treasure Hunt" and answer the questions asked below by choosing the correct option.

Multiple Choice Questions

What did Chip find buried near the rusty rig?

a) A shiny golden coin

b) A rusty old key

c) A treasure map

Which animals joined Chip on his treasure hunt?

a) Flip the horse, Kit the kitten, and Pip the chicken

b) Max the dog, Bella the bunny, and Ollie the owl

c) Sammy the squirrel, Lily the lamb, and Milo the mouse

What were some of the treasures they discovered along their journey?

a) Colorful figs, a silver locket, and a priceless ruby pendant

b) Shells, rocks, and feathers

c) Books, toys, and coins

How did Chip and his friends feel when they found the treasures?

a) Excited and amazed

b) Disappointed and bored

c) Scared and confused

What was the overall theme of the story?

a) Friendship and adventure

b) Greed and selfishness

c) Mystery and suspense

Read the story "Chip's Treasure Hunt" and solve the exercises given below.

Fill in the blanks

Chip's _____ nature often led him into trouble.

The rusty rig stood tall, surrounded by _____.

Chip stumbled upon a _____ buried in the ground.

Flip, Kit, and Pip were _____ who joined Chip on his adventure.

Along their journey, they discovered hidden _____.

Chip's heart raced with _____ as they uncovered each treasure.

The treasures they found filled them with a sense of _____.

Chip and his friends formed an unbreakable _____ during their quest.

The story reminded us of the importance of _____ and exploration.

In the end, Chip's treasure hunt proved that true wealth comes from _____.

True or False

Chip is a cautious and careful character in the story.	(True / False)
The rusty rig was surrounded by beautiful flowers.	(True / False)
Chip discovered a treasure chest buried in the ground.	(True / False)
Flip, Kit, and Pip are fictional characters in the story.	(True / False)
The treasures they found were all valuable and rare.	(True / False)
Chip's heart filled with fear as they uncovered each treasure.	(True / False)
The story emphasizes the importance of friendship and teamwork.	(True / False)
The moral of the story is that material possessions bring true happiness.	(True / False)

Read the story "Chip's Treasure Hunt" then read the statements written below and rewrite the correct statements.

Rewrite the correct statements.

Chip's cautious nature always kept him out of trouble.
_____

The rusty rig was surrounded by a pristine garden.
_____

Chip stumbled upon a pile of rocks buried in the ground.
_____

Flip, Kit, and Pip were imaginary characters who joined Chip on his adventure.
_____

Along their journey, they discovered ordinary, everyday objects.
_____

Chip's heart sank with disappointment as they uncovered each treasure.
_____

The treasures they found left them feeling unsatisfied and unfulfilled.
_____

Chip and his friends had constant conflicts and disagreements during their quest.
_____

The story reminded us that staying within our comfort zones is the key to happiness.
_____

In the end, Chip realized that material possessions are the only source of true wealth.
_____

Read the story and circle the 'ip' words. Write the 'ip' words in the box given below.

The Whimsical Trip

In a quaint little town, Kip had a peculiar habit of walking with a slight limp, which earned him the nickname "Lip." One sunny day, as Lip took a leisurely sip of his favorite tea, he noticed a shiny object on the ground. Curiosity got the better of him and he bent down to inspect it. Little did he know that this discovery would lead to an unexpected trip.

As he picked up the object, he realized it was a mysterious key. With a flip of his hand, Lip's hip accidentally brushed against a nearby ship's railing, causing the key to slip from his grip. The key hit the ground with a loud clip, and to Lip's surprise, a tiny door appeared.

With a drip of anticipation, Lip stepped through the door and found himself in a whimsical garden filled with colorful tulips. It was then that he noticed an old chest, equipped with a lock that matched the key he found.

With trembling hands, he inserted the key into the lock, turned it, and heard a satisfying click. The lid slowly opened, revealing a treasure that would forever change Lip's life. From that day forward, Lip's journey from a simple sip of tea to an extraordinary discovery became the stuff of legends.

Write all the 'ip' words found in the story.

Read the story "The Whimsical Trip" and answer the questions asked below.

Questions and Answers

What was the nickname given to the main character, and why did they have it?
_____
_____
_____

What led Lip to discover the mysterious key?
_____
_____
_____

How did Lip accidentally cause the key to slip from his grip?
_____
_____
_____

What awaited Lip on the other side of the tiny door?
_____
_____
_____

How did Lip's life change after unlocking the chest with the key?
_____
_____
_____

Read the story "The Whimsical Trip" and answer the questions asked below by choosing the correct option.

Multiple Choice Questions

What was the nickname given to the main character, Lip?

a) Slip

b) Kip

c) Skip

How did Lip discover the mysterious key?

a) He found it in a treasure chest

b) He stumbled upon it while walking

c) It was given to him by a friend

How did Lip accidentally cause the key to slip from his grip?

a) He tripped and dropped it

b) His hip brushed against a ship's railing

c) He flipped it in the air and couldn't catch it

What awaited Lip on the other side of the tiny door?

a) A magical forest

b) A secret garden filled with tulips

c) A hidden room with a treasure map

How did Lip's life change after unlocking the chest with the key?

a) He became famous overnight

b) He gained supernatural powers

c) His journey led to new adventures and discoveries

Read the story "The Whimsical Trip" and solve the exercises given below.

Fill in the blanks

The main character's nickname was _____.

Lip discovered the mysterious key while _____.

Unfortunately, Lip accidentally caused the key to slip from his grip when _____.

On the other side of the tiny door, Lip found himself in a _____.

The chest that Lip unlocked with the key contained _____.

Lip's journey with the key led him to encounter _____.

Along the way, Lip faced numerous _____.

In the end, Lip's adventures with the key taught him the importance of _____.

The key symbolized _____ for Lip.

Lip's life took a remarkable turn after unlocking the chest, leading to _____.

True or False

The main character's nickname was Slip. (T/ F)

Lip discovered the mysterious key while walking in the park. (T/ F)

Lip accidentally dropped the key when he tripped over a rock. (T/ F)

On the other side of the tiny door, Lip found himself in a magical forest. (T/ F)

The chest that Lip unlocked with the key contained a treasure map. (T/ F)

Lip's journey with the key led him to encounter mythical creatures. (T/ F)

Along the way, Lip faced numerous challenges and obstacles. (T/ F)

Lip's adventures with the key taught him the importance of perseverance. (T/ F)

Read the story "The Whimsical Trip" then read the statements written below and rewrite the correct statements.

Rewrite the correct statements.

In a bustling city, Kip had a normal habit of walking with a slight limp.
_____

Lip noticed a dull object on the ground while sipping his least favorite tea.
_____

Lip accidentally dropped the key and it made no sound as it hit the ground.
_____

Instead of a tiny door, a massive gate appeared after Lip dropped the key.
_____

Lip found himself in a gloomy garden filled with wilted flowers instead of colorful tulips.
_____

There was no chest with a matching lock for the key that Lip found.
_____

Lip inserted the key into the lock, but it got stuck and wouldn't turn.
_____

Instead of a treasure, the chest contained only old socks and empty wrappers.
_____

Lip's journey to an extraordinary discovery went unnoticed by everyone.
_____

Lip's story remained completely unknown and wasn't passed down as a legend.
_____

Read the story and circle the 'it' words. Write the 'it' words in the box given below.

The Knitting Master

Once upon a time, in a small village, there lived a skilled tailor named Evan. He was known for his ability to knit exquisite garments. One sunny day, as Evan sat in his humble cottage, he received an unexpected visit from a traveler seeking a special kit for knitting. The traveler admired Evan's talent and wanted to learn the craft.

Impressed by the traveler's enthusiasm, Evan agreed to provide him with a kit. As they sat together, Evan explained the different types of needles that fit best for various garments. The traveler eagerly listened and absorbed every bit of information.

As Evan shared his knowledge, he realized that teaching was his true calling. He decided to admit the traveler into his apprentice program, offering him a chance to learn the trade formally. The traveler gladly accepted the invitation.

Months passed, and the apprentice's skills grew. Evan took pride in seeing his student's progress. Eventually, the apprentice became a master knitter in his own right, giving credit to Evan's guidance.

Evan's decision to quit his solitary habit of knitting alone had brought him joy, fulfillment, and the opportunity to shape a new generation of skilled artisans. It was a decision that he would never regret.

Write all the 'it' words found in the story.

Read the story "The Knitting Master" and answer the questions asked below.

Questions and Answers

What was the special kit that the traveler sought from Evan?

_____
_____
_____

How did Evan feel when he realized that teaching was his true calling?

_____
_____
_____

What did Evan decide to do after seeing the progress of his apprentice?

_____
_____
_____

How did Evan's decision to quit his solitary habit impact his life?

_____
_____
_____

What was the legacy that Evan left behind as a knitting master?

_____
_____
_____

Read the story "The Knitting Master" and answer the questions asked below by choosing the correct option.

Multiple Choice Questions

What was the skill for which Evan was known in the small village?

a) Carpentry

b) Knitting

c) Pottery

What did the traveler seek from Evan?

a) A recipe for a special dish

b) A kit for knitting

c) Guidance on farming techniques

How did Evan feel when he realized teaching was his true calling?

a) Regretful

b) Fulfilled

c) Indifferent

What did Evan offer the traveler after realizing his passion for teaching?

a) An invitation to join his apprentice program

b) A voucher for a local restaurant

c) A free knitting book

What impact did Evan's decision to quit his solitary habit have on his life?

a) It made him lonelier

b) It brought him joy and fulfillment

c) It caused financial difficulties

Read the story "The Knitting Master" and solve the exercises given below.

Fill in the blanks

Evan was known as the _____ in the small village.

The traveler sought a special _____ from Evan.

Evan realized that his true calling was _____.

After seeing the progress of his apprentice, Evan decided to quit his _____ habit.

Evan's decision to teach knitting had a profound impact on his _____.

The legacy that Evan left behind was that of a skilled and dedicated _____.

The special kit that the traveler sought was said to contain _____.

Evan's newfound passion for teaching brought him _____ and fulfillment.

The village community admired Evan's _____ skills and dedication.

True or False

Evan was known for his knitting skills in the small village. (T/ F)

The traveler sought guidance on farming techniques from Evan. (T/ F)

Evan realized that teaching was his true passion after meeting the traveler. (T/ F)

Evan decided to continue his solitary habit. (T/ F)

Evan's decision to teach knitting had a positive impact on his life. (T/ F)

The special kit that the traveler sought contained a recipe for a special dish. (T/ F)

Evan's newfound passion for teaching brought him fulfillment and joy. (T/ F)

The village community admired Evan for his pottery skills. (T/ F)

Read the story "The Knitting Master" then read the statements written below and rewrite the correct statements.

Rewrite the correct statements.

Evan was known as the best fisherman in the small village.
_____

The traveler sought a rare gemstone from Evan.
_____

Evan realized that his true calling was professional wrestling.
_____

After seeing the progress of his apprentice, Evan decided to give up on teaching.
_____

Evan's decision to teach knitting had a negative impact on his life.
_____

The special kit that the traveler sought contained a magic wand.
_____

Evan's newfound passion for teaching brought him frustration and disappointment.
_____

The village community admired Evan for his exceptional singing skills.
_____

Evan's solitary habit involved collecting seashells on the beach.
_____

Evan's decision to share his knowledge and skills brought about no change in his life.
_____

Use the words given below in your own sentences.

Sentences

Lip: _____

Hip: _____

Tip: _____

Sip: _____

Clip: _____

Trip: _____

Flip: _____

Lit: _____

Kit: _____

Bit: _____

Sit: _____

Fit: _____

Knit: _____

Nib: _____

Rib: _____

Pin: _____

Win: _____

Tin: _____

Identify the picture and write its name.

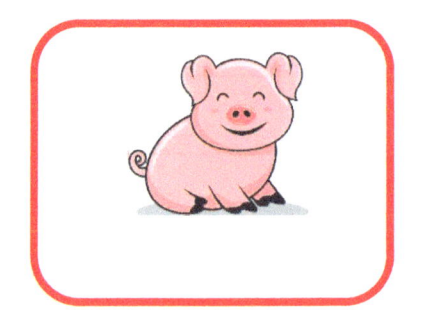

Match the picture to its name.

Clip

Twig

Pin

Lip

Ship

Sit

Dig

Hit

Fig

Knit

Pig

Rig

Complete the word by looking at the picture.

👄	l			
🚢	sh			
🧍	s			
🛢️	r			
🐷	p			
🧶	kn			
🧒	h			
🍈	f			

Find and circle the words written below.

fig dig big rig pin sin fin lip hip
tip trip clip ship

c	t	r	i	p	a	l	l
l	e	a	t	e	f	i	n
i	s	h	i	p	y	p	g
p	w	i	e	r	h	i	p
s	g	a	m	s	l	g	e
b	i	a	g	e	s	j	n
i	r	d	i	g	p	i	e
g	b	e	f	l	p	t	n

Read the story and circle the 'o' words. Write the 'o' words in the box given below.

Reaching for the Stars

Once upon a time, there was a brave and curious dog named Bob. Bob lived in a small town where nothing exciting ever happened. One day, Bob gathered his friends, a hog, a frog, and a log, and shared an extraordinary idea with them. He wanted to embark on an adventure to space!

With determination in their eyes, the unlikely group of friends built a rocket from scratch. They worked day and night, facing challenges and overcoming obstacles. Finally, the day arrived when they were ready for liftoff.

As they soared through the clouds, the fog cleared, revealing the breathtaking view of Earth from above. The temperature inside the rocket became hot, but the friends were not deterred. They marveled at the wonders of the universe, floating weightlessly like an ox in zero gravity.

They hopped from planet to planet, exploring alien landscapes and encountering bizarre creatures. With their trusty mop and broom, they cleaned up space debris, leaving each planet spotless.

After a lot of excitement and discovery, it was time to return home. Bob and his friends landed safely. Their incredible journey had not only brought them closer together but also inspired others to dream big and reach for the stars.

Write all the 'o' words found in the story.

Read the story "Reaching for the Stars" and answer the questions asked below.

Questions and Answers

Who was the brave and curious protagonist of the story?
_____
_____
_____

Which unlikely group of friends joined Bob on his space adventure?
_____
_____
_____

How did Bob and his friends overcome the challenges they faced while building the rocket?
_____
_____
_____

What did Bob and his friends encounter as they hopped from planet to planet in space?
_____
_____
_____

How did Bob's incredible journey inspire others in the small town?
_____
_____

Read the story "Reaching for the Stars" and answer the questions asked below by choosing the correct option.

Multiple Choice Questions

What was the name of the brave and curious dog in the story?

a) Max

b) Bob

c) Sam

Who were Bob's friends who joined him on the space adventure?

a) Cat, Mouse, and Bird

b) Hog, Frog, and Log

c) Rabbit, Squirrel, and Turtle

How did Bob and his friends overcome the challenges while building the rocket?

a) They asked for help from their parents.

b) They worked together and persevered.

c) They gave up and abandoned the idea.

What did Bob and his friends encounter as they explored different planets?

a) Friendly aliens and new civilizations

b) Wild animals and dangerous terrains

c) Empty and lifeless landscapes

How did Bob's incredible journey inspire others in the small town?

a) They organized a celebration in Bob's honor.

b) They started dreaming big and pursuing their own adventures.

c) They forgot about Bob's adventure quickly and moved on.

Read the story "Reaching for the Stars" and solve the exercises given below.

Fill in the blanks

Bob was a _____ and _____ protagonist of the story.

In order to reach the stars, Bob and his friends built a _____.

Along their journey, Bob and his friends faced many _____.

Despite the difficulties, Bob and his friends remained _____ and _____.

As they hopped from planet to planet, Bob and his friends encountered _____ and _____ creatures.

The incredible journey of Bob inspired the people in the small town to dream _____ and _____.

Bob's adventure taught everyone the importance of _____ and _____.

The town organized a _____ to celebrate Bob's achievements.

Bob's story spread far and wide, inspiring others to embark on their own _____.

True or False

The protagonist of the story was a brave and curious dog named Bob.   (True / False)

Bob and his friends built a rocket to travel to space.   (True / False)

Bob and his friends easily overcame all the challenges they faced while building the rocket.   (True / False)

Bob's incredible journey inspired the people in the small town to dream big. (True / False)

The people in organized a celebration in honor of Bob's achievements.   (True / False)

Bob's story was quickly forgotten by everyone in the small town.   (True / False)

Through perseverance and teamwork, Bob and his friends proved that anything is possible.   (True / False)

Read the story "Reaching for the Stars", read the statements written below and rewrite the correct statements.

Rewrite the correct statements.

Bob was a cat, not a dog, in the story.
_____

Instead of building a rocket, Bob and his friends constructed a submarine to explore the deep sea.
_____

The challenges faced by Bob and his friends were minimal and easily overcome.
_____

Bob's incredible journey did not inspire anyone in the small town; it went unnoticed by the townspeople.
_____

Bob's story became a local legend, with people talking about it for generations.
_____

Through laziness and lack of coordination, Bob and his friends failed in their endeavors.
_____

Bob and his friends realized that dreaming big was pointless and focused on leading ordinary lives.
_____

Despite their efforts, Bob and his friends never succeeded in proving that anything is possible
_____

Read the story and circle the 'ot' words. Write the 'ot' words in the box given below.

Summer Adventure

Once upon a time, in a small town, there lived a baby named Timmy and his kind-hearted babysitter, Sarah. It was a scorching hot summer day, and Sarah decided to take Timmy to the park to cool off. As they strolled along, they noticed a group of children playing near a fountain. Timmy's eyes lit up with excitement.

Sarah found a shady spot under a tree and sat down, holding Timmy on her lap. Timmy giggled as he watched the children splashing in the water. Suddenly, Sarah noticed a strange smell. She quickly realized that Timmy had a runny nose, and it had turned into a snot-filled mess.

Determined not to let a little snot ruin their day, Sarah grabbed a tissue from her bag and gently wiped Timmy's nose. Timmy gurgled happily, grateful for Sarah's care. Sarah jotted down the incident in her notebook, making a mental note to bring extra tissues next time.

As the sun began to set, Sarah packed up their things and headed home. Timmy's runny nose became a distant memory as they chatted about their adventures in the park. With Sarah by his side, Timmy felt safe and loved, knowing he had a babysitter who always got him out of sticky situations.

Write all the 'ot' words found in the story.

Read the story "Summer Adventure" and answer the questions asked below.

Questions and Answers

Who is the main character in the story?
_____
_____
_____

What did Sarah decide to do on the hot summer day?
_____
_____
_____

Where did Sarah and Timmy find a shady spot to sit?
_____
_____
_____

What caused Timmy's nose to become runny?
_____
_____
_____

What did Sarah do to help Timmy with his runny nose?
_____
_____
_____

Read the story "Summer Adventure" and answer the questions asked below by choosing the correct option.

Multiple Choice Questions

What did Timmy and Sarah do on the hot summer day?

a) Went to the beach

b) Went to the park

c) Stayed indoors

Where did Sarah find a shady spot to sit with Timmy?

a) Under a tree

b) Near a fountain

c) On a bench

What caused Timmy's nose to become runny?

a) The scorching heat

b) Playing in the water

c) Eating ice cream

How did Sarah clean Timmy's runny nose?

a) She used a tissue

b) She used her sleeve

c) She used a handkerchief

How did Timmy feel after Sarah wiped his nose?

a) Grateful

b) Annoyed

c) Indifferent

Read the story "Summer Adventure" and solve the exercises given below.

Fill in the blanks

Timmy and Sarah decided to spend their _____ day outdoors.

The sun was shining brightly, making it a _____ summer day.

Sarah suggested finding a shady spot to sit and _____.

They found a comfortable spot _____ a large tree.

As they sat down, Timmy noticed his nose was starting to _____.

Sarah quickly rummaged through her bag and found a _____.

She handed the tissue to Timmy and gently wiped his _____.

Timmy felt relieved as the tissue absorbed the _____ from his nose.

Sarah laughed and said, "Looks like your nose is no longer _____!"

They continued enjoying their day, grateful for the shade and _____ company.

True or False

The story takes place on a hot summer day.	(True / False)
Timmy and Sarah decided to stay indoors on the hot day.	(True / False)
They found a shady spot under a tree to sit.	(True / False)
Timmy's nose became runny because of the scorching heat.	(True / False)
Sarah used her sleeve to clean Timmy's runny nose.	(True / False)
Timmy felt grateful after Sarah wiped his nose.	(True / False)
Sarah suggested finding a sunny spot to sit and play.	(True / False)
They spent the day at the beach enjoying the water.	(True / False)

Read the story "Summer Adventure" then read the statements written below and rewrite the correct statements.

Rewrite the correct statements.

Timmy and Sarah decided to spend their rainy day outdoors.
_____

The sun was shining brightly, making it a cool winter day.
_____

Sarah suggested finding a sunny spot to sit and play.
_____

They found a comfortable spot under a small shrub.
_____

As they sat down, Timmy noticed his nose was starting to itch.
_____

Sarah quickly rummaged through her bag and found a toy.
_____

She handed the toy to Timmy and gently wiped his face.
_____

Timmy felt annoyed as the toy didn't help with his runny nose.
_____

Sarah laughed and said, "Looks like your nose is still runny!"
_____

They continued enjoying their day at the library, surrounded by books.
_____

Read the story and circle the 'op' words. Write the 'op' words in the box given below.

The Donut Hero

Once upon a time, in a bustling city, there was a cop named Charlie. He was known for his impeccable sense of justice and his love for donuts. Every morning, Charlie would visit his favorite donut shop at the top of the hill. With a hop in his step, he would enter the shop and order a dozen freshly baked donuts.

One day, as Charlie was enjoying his favorite treat, he received an urgent call on his radio. There was a robbery in progress at the convenience store down the street. Without hesitation, Charlie quickly finished his donut, dropped some cash on the counter, and dashed out of the shop.

As he reached the scene, he saw the suspect attempting to flee. With a swift move, Charlie lunged forward and made a spectacular tackle, causing the thief to flop onto the ground. The stolen items, including a bag of crop seeds, fell from the thief's hands.

With the situation under control, Charlie apprehended the robber and returned to the donut shop. The news of his heroic act had spread like wildfire, and the shop owner presented him with a special donut, topped with a shiny gold badge-shaped prop.

Charlie proudly accepted the honor, enjoying his reward while the locals cheered with joy. From that day on, the tale of the cop with a love for donuts became a popular story in the city.

Write all the 'op' words found in the story.

Read the story "The Donut Hero" and answer the questions asked below.

Questions and Answers

Who is the protagonist of the story?
_____
_____
_____

What is the cop known for besides his sense of justice?
_____
_____
_____

Where is the cop's favorite donut shop located?
_____
_____
_____

What interrupts the cop's peaceful morning at the donut shop?
_____
_____
_____

How does the cop handle the situation and what does he receive as a reward?
_____
_____
_____

Read the story "The Donut Hero" and answer the questions asked below by choosing the correct option.

Multiple Choice Questions

What is the definition of a story?

a) A piece of prose fiction

b) An account of incidents or events

c) A description of connected series of events

What is Storyline Online?

a) A Kansas City restaurant

b) A website featuring actors reading children's books

c) A platform for sharing life-changing stories

What is a short story?

a) A narrative focusing on self-contained incidents

b) A report of connected series of events

c) A piece of poetry that can be read in a single sitting

What is the common use of the term "story"?

a) A description of real or imaginary people and events

b) A restaurant located in Prairie Village, KS

c) A type of short film typically shown in theaters

What is the purpose of StoryCorps?

a) Sharing moral stories for kids

b) Changing the way people listen to stories

c) Offering a platform for reading free children's stories

Read the story "The Donut Hero" and solve the exercises given below.

Fill in the blanks

The sun shone brightly overhead, casting a warm _____ over the meadow.

Sarah skipped through the tall grass, her laughter echoing through the _____.

As she reached the edge of the meadow, Sarah spotted a colorful _____ perched on a branch.

The bird chirped a melodic tune, filling the air with its joyful _____.

Sarah's eyes widened in awe as she watched the bird spread its wings and take _____.

She felt a sense of _____ as she observed the bird's graceful flight.

Sarah wished she could soar through the sky like the bird, feeling the wind against her _____.

Sarah closed her eyes and breathed in deeply, savoring the sweet fragrance of the _____.

True or False

The protagonist of the story is a police officer named Officer Johnson. (T / F)

The donut shop in the story is famous for its savory sandwiches. (T / F)

Officer Johnson enjoyed a cup of tea at the donut shop every morning. (T / F)

The troublemakers in the story were causing a disturbance near the donut shop. (T / F)

Officer Johnson hesitated before taking action to apprehend the troublemakers. (T / F)

The donut shop owner rewarded Officer Johnson with a free meal as a token of gratitude. (T / F)

The local newspaper covered Officer Johnson's heroic act. (T / F)

The community showed their appreciation for Officer Johnson. (T / F)

Read the story "The Donut Hero" then read the statements written below and rewrite the correct statements.

Rewrite the correct statements.

The protagonist of the story is a firefighter named Officer Johnson.
_____

The donut shop in the story is known for its spicy tacos.
_____

Officer Johnson enjoyed a cup of lemonade at the donut shop every morning.
_____

The troublemakers in the story were causing a disturbance in a library.
_____

Officer Johnson hesitated for a long time before taking action to apprehend the troublemakers.
_____

The donut shop owner rewarded Officer Johnson with a new car as a token of gratitude.
_____

The local newspaper ignored Officer Johnson's heroic act and it went unnoticed.
_____

Sarah, the protagonist, had a fear of birds and ran away when she spotted one.
_____

The meadow was filled with thorny bushes and there were no grassy areas.
_____

Use the words given below in your own sentences.

Sentences

Job: _____

Cob: _____

Rob: _____

Knob: _____

Crop: _____

Hop: _____

Shop: _____

Top: _____

Crop: _____

Flop: _____

Hot: _____

Not: _____

Cot: _____

Got: _____

Rot: _____

Hog: _____

Dog: _____

Fog: _____

Identify the picture and write its name.

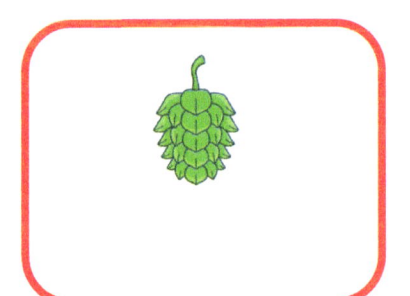

Match the picture to its name.

Shop

Cop

Frog

Dog

Hob

Hot

Sob

Cob

Hop

Log

Hog

Pot

Complete the word by looking at the picture.

	fr			
	sh			
	l			
	p			
	h			
	h			
	c			
	d			

Find and circle the words written below.

hog   dog   fog   jog   hob   knob   sob   rob
hot   got   knot   lot

c	s	o	b	p	a	h	r
t	e	k	t	e	f	o	o
o	s	n	i	p	y	t	b
l	h	b	e	r	h	i	g
g	o	a	m	s	g	t	o
o	b	a	g	o	o	o	t
j	r	d	h	g	d	n	e
g	f	o	g	l	p	k	n

Read the story and circle the 'u' words. Write the 'u' words in the box given below.

Bound by Mud

Once upon a sunny day, in a small village nestled among the rolling hills, there lived a young boy named Bud. Bud loved to have fun, especially when he could run and play in the warm sun. One day, while exploring near the riverbank, he stumbled upon a patch of sticky mud. With a loud thud, Bud's foot got stuck, and he couldn't move a stud.

Just as Bud was beginning to worry, he heard a soft voice. It was the village nun, who had come to shun away from the chaos of the world. She quickly untangled Bud's foot, leaving him stunned. Grateful for her help, Bud offered to fetch her a cup of tea.

As Bud ran back to the village, he noticed a pup chasing its tail near the old hut. His heart full of joy, Bud decided to bring the pup along. When they arrived at the nun's humble abode, she was surprised to see the little companion Bud had brought.

From that day on, Bud, the pup, and the nun became inseparable. They would spend their days playing, laughing, and basking in the warm sun, creating memories that would never be forgotten. And in the end, what started as a muddy mishap turned into a beautiful tale of friendship and love.

Write all the 'u' words found in the story.

Read the story "Bound by Mud" and answer the questions asked below.

Questions and Answers

Who was the young boy in the story, and what did he love to do?
___
___
___

What unexpected obstacle did Bud encounter while exploring near the riverbank?
___
___
___

How did the nun come to Bud's rescue?
___
___
___

What gesture of gratitude did Bud make towards the nun?
___
___
___

How did Bud, the pup, and the nun spend their days together after their initial encounter?
___
___
___

Read the story "Bound by Mud" and answer the questions asked below by choosing the correct option.

Multiple Choice Questions

What was the name of the young boy in the story?

a) Tom

b) Bud

c) Max

Where did Bud stumble upon a patch of sticky mud?

a) Playground

b) Forest

c) Riverbank

Who came to Bud's rescue when his foot got stuck?

a) The village nun

b) A friendly neighbor

c) His pet dog

What did Bud offer to bring the nun as a gesture of gratitude?

a) A cup of tea

b) A plate of cookies

c) A bouquet of flowers

How did Bud, the pup, and the nun spend their days together?

a) Painting and drawing

b) Singing and dancing

c) Playing and laughing

Read the story "Bound by Mud" and solve the exercises given below.

Fill in the blanks

The young boy's name was ___.

Bud loved to explore the ___ near the riverbank.

Bud got his foot stuck in a patch of ___.

The village ___ came to Bud's rescue.

As a gesture of gratitude, Bud offered to bring the nun a cup of ___.

Bud, the pup, and the nun spent their days together ___ and laughing.

The story took place in a peaceful ___.

Bud's encounter with the nun taught him the importance of ___.

The muddy adventure brought ___ to Bud's life.

Bud's love for exploration led him on ___ adventures in the future.

True or False

Bud was a young girl in the story. (True / False)

Bud loved to explore the forest near the riverbank. (True / False)

Bud's foot got stuck in a patch of quicksand. (True / False)

A friendly neighbor came to Bud's rescue. (True / False)

Bud offered to bring the nun a cup of tea as a gesture of gratitude. (True / False)

Bud, the pup, and the nun spent their days together playing and laughing. (True / False)

The story took place in a bustling city. (True / False)

Bud's encounter with the nun taught him the importance of kindness. (True / False)

Read the story "Bound by Mud" then read the statements written below and rewrite the correct statements.

Rewrite the correct statements.

The young boy's name was Tim.
_____

Bud loved to explore the mountains near the riverbank.
_____

Bud got his foot stuck in a patch of quicksand.
_____

The village doctor came to Bud's rescue.
_____

As a gesture of gratitude, Bud offered to bring the nun a plate of cookies.
_____

Bud, the pup, and the nun spent their days together painting and drawing.
_____

The story took place in a chaotic city.
_____

Bud's encounter with the nun taught him the importance of bravery.
_____

The muddy adventure brought sadness to Bud's life.
_____

Bud's love for exploration led him on dangerous adventures in the future.
_____

Read the story and circle the 'un' words. Write the 'un' words in the box given below.

Sunville's Stunned Savior

In the small town of Sunville, the sun shone brightly as the annual Fun Fair began. Families gathered to enjoy the festivities, munching on warm buns while children ran around laughing and playing. Among the crowd was a mysterious nun, who seemed out of place in her traditional habit.

As the day progressed, excitement filled the air. Suddenly, a loud bang echoed through the fairgrounds. Panic ensued as people realized a gun had been fired. Everyone scattered, trying to escape the danger. The nun, however, stood her ground, her eyes focused and determined.

In a remarkable display of bravery, she swiftly spun around, reaching out her hand towards the running crowd. Miraculously, time seemed to freeze as a powerful force emanated from her palm, temporarily stunning the assailant. The crowd watched in awe as the threat was neutralized.

The nun's courage and quick thinking saved the day, turning what could have been a tragedy into a tale of heroism. The town of Sunville would forever remember the day when a nun stunned danger and spun it away, preserving their fun-filled fair.

Write all the 'ot' words found in the story.

Read the story "Sunville's Stunned Savior" and answer the questions asked below.

Questions and Answers

Who is the mysterious nun and why is she at the Fun Fair?
_____
_____
_____

What events led up to the moment when the gun was fired?
_____
_____
_____

How did the nun manage to stun the assailant and save the day?
_____
_____
_____

How did the crowd react to the nun's display of bravery?
_____
_____
_____

Will the town of Sunville hold the annual Fun Fair again next year after the incident?
_____
_____
_____

Read the story "Sunville's Stunned Savior" and answer the questions asked below by choosing the correct option.

Multiple Choice Questions

What was the annual event happening in Sunville?

a) Fun Fair

b) Music Festival

c) Art Exhibition

Who stood her ground during the incident at the Fun Fair?

a) A mysterious nun

b) A police officer

c) A magician

How did the nun save the day?

a) By freezing time

b) By calling for backup

c) By performing a magic trick

What was the reaction of the crowd to the nun's actions?

a) Awe and admiration

b) Fear and confusion

c) Indifference and boredom

Will the town of Sunville continue to host the Fun Fair in the future?

a) Yes

b) No

c) Uncertain

Read the story "Sunville's Stunned Savior" and solve the exercises given below.

Fill in the blanks

The mysterious nun's presence at the _____ intrigued everyone.

As the _____ gathered around the main stage, a sense of excitement filled the air.

Suddenly, chaos erupted when a _____ echoed through the fairgrounds.

People screamed and _____ in all directions, desperately seeking safety.

In the midst of the panic, the _____ remained calm and composed.

With swift and precise movements, she approached the _____, who was holding a gun.

Using some unknown power or skill, she _____ him, rendering him unable to harm anyone else.

The _____ watched in awe and disbelief as the situation unfolded before their eyes.

The local _____ arrived shortly after, taking the stunned assailant into custody.

True or False

The Fun Fair was an annual event in Sunville. (True / False)

The mysterious nun's presence at the Fun Fair raised suspicions. (True / False)

The incident at the Fun Fair involved the firing of a gun. (True / False)

The nun showed bravery and courage during the chaotic situation. (True / False)

The crowd reacted with fear and confusion when the gunshot rang out. (True / False)

The nun used a special power or skill to incapacitate the assailant. (True / False)

The local police arrived quickly to apprehend the assailant. (True / False)

The nun disappeared without a trace, leaving the crowd in awe and wonder. (True / False)

Read the story "Sunville's Stunned Savior" then read the statements written below and rewrite the correct statements.

Rewrite the correct statements.

The Fun Fair was a monthly event held in Sunville.

The mysterious nun's presence at the Fun Fair went unnoticed by everyone.

_____

The incident at the Fun Fair involved the release of a swarm of bees.

_____

The nun panicked and ran away when the chaos erupted.

_____

The crowd remained calm and composed during the chaotic situation.

_____

The assailant managed to escape before the nun could take any action.

_____

The onlookers were unimpressed and bored by the nun's actions.

_____

The local police arrived late, allowing the assailant to flee.

_____

The nun revealed herself to be a regular magician performing a trick.

_____

The nun left behind a sense of disappointment and resentment among the crowd.

_____

Read the story and circle the 'ug' words. Write the 'ug' words in the box given below.

The Magical Jug

Once upon a time, in a quaint little town, there lived a young girl named Lily. Lily loved exploring the outdoors and had a special fondness for bugs. One sunny afternoon, while playing in her backyard, she stumbled upon a small ladybug. Delighted, she gently picked it up and gave it a hug.

As Lily continued her adventures, she noticed a colorful rug lying nearby. Curiosity got the better of her, and she knelt down to examine it. To her surprise, she discovered a hidden compartment beneath the rug. With excitement, she dug deeper and found an old jug.

Lily couldn't resist her curiosity and decided to investigate further. As she tugged at the jug's lid, a peculiar aroma filled the air. Perplexed, she shrugged her shoulders, wondering what it could be. Little did she know that hidden inside was a magical potion, rumored to grant extraordinary powers.

Without thinking twice, she drank a drop from the jug. Suddenly, she felt energized and experienced a surge of strength. She realized the power she held within and knew she had found something truly special. With her newfound abilities, Lily went on to become the town's hero, using her powers for good. And all because of a bug, a hug, and the mysterious jug she had discovered.

Write all the 'ug' words found in the story.

Read the story "The Magical Jug" and answer the questions asked below.

Questions and Answers

What did Lily discover hidden beneath the colorful rug in her backyard?
_____
_____
_____

How did Lily feel when she stumbled upon the small ladybug?
_____
_____
_____

What did Lily decide to do with the jug she found?
_____
_____
_____

What happened to Lily after she drank a drop from the jug?
_____
_____
_____

How did Lily use her newfound powers to become a hero in her town?
_____
_____
_____

Read the story "The Magical Jug" and answer the questions asked below by choosing the correct option.

Multiple Choice Questions

What did Lily find hidden beneath the rug in her backyard?

a) A hidden treasure

b) A small ladybug

c) A magical potion

How did Lily feel when she discovered the hidden compartment?

a) Surprised and curious

b) Scared and frightened

c) Indifferent and uninterested

What happened to Lily after she drank a drop from the jug?

a) She became invisible

b) She gained super strength

c) Nothing happened, it was just a regular jug

How did Lily use her newfound powers?

a) To fly and explore the world

b) To become a superhero and help others

c) To perform magic tricks for entertainment

What was the town's reaction to Lily's powers?

a) They feared her and thought she was dangerous

b) They celebrated her as a local hero

c) They were indifferent and uninterested in her abilities

Read the story "The Magical Jug" and solve the exercises given below.

Fill in the blanks

Lily was amazed when she discovered a _____ beneath the colorful rug in her backyard.

The small ladybug had vibrant _____ spots on its wings.

Lily decided to keep the jug as a _____ of her magical find.

After drinking a drop from the jug, Lily felt a surge of _____ coursing through her veins.

With her newfound powers, Lily could _____ objects with just a touch.

Lily's best friend, Alex, was _____ by her incredible abilities.

The townspeople couldn't believe their eyes when they saw Lily _____ through the air.

Lily used her powers to _____ a group of kittens stuck in a tree.

True or False

Lily found the hidden compartment beneath the rug in her backyard. (True / False)

The small ladybug had colorful spots on its wings. (True / False)

Lily decided to sell the jug she found for a large sum of money. (True / False)

After drinking from the jug, Lily gained extraordinary powers. (True / False)

Lily used her powers to become a mischievous troublemaker in her town. (True / False)

The townspeople were amazed and grateful for Lily's heroic deeds. (True / False)

Lily's best friend, Alex, was jealous of her newfound abilities. (True / False)

Lily learned that having powers came with great responsibility. (True / False)

Read the story "The Magical Jug", read the statements written below and rewrite the correct statements.

Rewrite the correct statements.

Lily found the hidden compartment beneath the rug in her front yard.
_____

The small ladybug had black spots on its wings.
_____

Lily decided to throw away the jug she found as it seemed useless.
_____

After drinking from the jug, Lily lost all her powers.
_____

Lily used her powers to cause chaos and destruction in her town.
_____

The townspeople were terrified and angry at Lily for her actions.
_____

Lily's best friend, Alex, was supportive and proud of her newfound abilities.
_____

Lily learned that having powers meant she could do whatever she wanted.
_____

Lily discovered that her powers only worked during the daytime.
_____

The mysterious jug was actually just an ordinary water container.
_____

Use the words given below in your own sentences.

Sentences

Rug: _____

Jug: _____

Bug: _____

Hug: _____

Rug: _____

Mug: _____

Shrug: _____

Dug: _____

Bun: _____

Fun: _____

Sun: _____

Nun: _____

Shun: _____

Run: _____

Hut: _____

Shut: _____

Cut: _____

Nut: _____

Identify the picture and write its name.

Match the picture to its name.

Sun

Drug

Hug

Hut

Run

Nun

Bug

Nut

Rug

Cut

Bun

Jug

Complete the word by looking at the picture.

	h			
	n			
	b			
	n			
	r			
	c			
	j			
	s			

Find and circle the words written below.

cut hut nut but shut nun bun
sun fun gun bug hug rug dug

f	u	n	g	p	g	h	r
t	h	k	t	u	f	o	b
o	u	g	u	d	n	t	u
l	g	u	e	r	h	i	n
g	h	r	t	s	g	t	o
n	b	u	g	o	b	u	n
u	c	d	t	g	u	h	u
s	f	o	n	u	t	s	n

Made in the USA
Monee, IL
20 March 2025